Heartbroken:
Thoughts on Loss

Heartbroken:

Thoughts on Loss

Edited by Lynne Widli

BARNES
& NOBLE
BOOKS

NEW YORK

The quotes in this book have been drawn from many sources, and are assumed to be accurate as quoted in their previously published forms. Although every effort has been made to verify the quotes and sources, the publisher cannot guarantee their perfect accuracy.

Introduction

NONE OF US WILL ESCAPE HEARTBREAK DURING OUR lifetime. And as Mark Twain points out, "Nothing that grieves us can be called little: by the eternal laws of proportion a child's loss of a doll and a king's loss of a crown are events of the same size."

You may not be a crownless king, but you have surely been on the wrong end of a love affair gone bad. You've probably known the grief that comes with the death of a loved one. You've wondered if a lonely, miserable day will ever end and you remember still the passing of your first childhood pet.

We can all catalogue many such unhappinesses. I myself have lost two fiancés, two jobs and two pearl earrings, which pretty well covers the entire range of proportion from insignificant to unbearable. In compiling this collection of quotations I looked for words which would reflect my own experiences as a person like you; someone all too well-acquainted with the ups and downs of human existence.

The quotes are organized to show the arc of grief, as I remember it: Bad things happen. You feel as if you cannot go on. Your friends and family rally to support you (or not). You cry and cry. The days seem bleak and endless. And then, slowly, a little laugh or two or three begins to sneak in. And you wake up one morning to find that you have endured.

These words are not meant to be a panacea, but perhaps they can offer at least the comfort of knowing that we all have had broken hearts and that the mending of them begins with knowing that we're not in it alone.

Sorrow comes unsent for…

It is God's giving if we laugh or weep.

—SOPHOCLES, *Ajax*

There are as many nights as days, and the one is just as long as the other in the year's course. Even a happy life cannot be without a measure of darkness and the word 'happy' would lose its meaning if it were not balanced by sadness.

—CARL JUNG

This is courage in a man:
To bear unflinchingly what heaven sends.

–EURIPIDES, *Heracles*

What is deservedly suffered must be borne with calmness, but when the pain is unmerited, the grief is resistless.

–OVID

A torn jacket is soon mended; but hard words bruise the heart of a child.

–HENRY WADSWORTH LONGFELLOW,
"Table-Talk," *Driftwood*

Sorrow comes unsent for.

–JOHN RAY, *A Collection of English Proverbs*

How small and selfish is sorrow. But it bangs one about until one is senseless.

—ELIZABETH, THE QUEEN MOTHER, in a letter to Edith Sitwell, shortly after the death of George VI

People forget the good, because the bad has more punch.

—LOUISE ERDRICH, *The Bingo Palace*

Now and then there is a person born who is so unlucky that he runs into accidents which started out to happen to somebody else.

—DON MARQUIS, American humorist

The bad end unhappily, the good unluckily. That is what tragedy means.

—TOM STOPPARD, playwright

Pain was not given thee merely to be miserable under; learn from it, turn it to account.

—THOMAS CARLYLE, from his journal.

Human kind
Cannot bear very much reality.

—T. S. ELIOT, *Four Quartets*

Reality cannot be ignored except at a price; and the longer the ignorance is persisted in, the higher and the more terrible becomes the price that must be paid.

—ALDOUS HUXLEY, *Vedanta For the Western World*

In a real dark night of the soul it is always three o'clock in the morning, day after day.

—F. SCOTT FITZGERALD, *The Crack-Up*

In moments of despair, we look on ourselves leadenly as objects...

—MARY McCARTHY, *On the Contrary*

Things are going to get a lot worse before they get worse.

—LILY TOMLIN

O insupportable and touching loss!

My God, my God, why hast thou forsaken me?
—BIBLE, *Psalms 22:1*

When we lose one we love, our bitterest tears are called forth by the memory of hours when we loved not enough.

—MAURICE MAETERLINCK, *Wisdom and Destiny*

When you're 50 you start thinking about things you haven't thought about before. I used to think getting old was about vanity—but actually it's about losing people you love. Getting wrinkles is trivial.

—JOYCE CAROL OATES

It often happens that the real tragedies of life occur in such an inartistic manner that they hurt us by their crude violence, their absolute incoherence, their absurd want of meaning, their entire lack of style.

—OSCAR WILDE

Only in the agony of parting do we look into the depths of love.

—GEORGE ELIOT

The death of a mother is the first sorrow wept without her.

—Anonymous

Heap not on this mound
Roses that she loved so well;
Why bewilder her with roses,
That she cannot see or smell?

—Edna St. Vincent Millay, "Epitaph," *Second April*

There was and still is the great disaster of my life—that lovely, lovely little boy.... There's no tragedy in life like the death of a child. Things never get back to the way they were.

—Dwight D. Eisenhower

My son, a perfect little boy of five years and three months, had ended his earthly life. You can never sympathize with me; you can never know how much of me such a young child can take away. A few weeks ago I accounted myself a very rich man, and now the poorest of all.

—RALPH WALDO EMERSON,
in a letter to Thomas Carlyle.

"Major, tell my father I died with my face to the enemy."

—I. E. AVERY, Confederate Colonel,
Battle of Gettysburg

The light has gone out of my life.

—THEODORE ROOSEVELT, in his diary, on the death of
his wife Alice Lee

Not louder shrieks to pitying heaven are cast,
When husbands, or when lapdogs breathe
    their last.

—ALEXANDER POPE, *The Rape of the Lock*

Sometimes, when one person is missing, the whole
world seems depopulated.

—ALPHONSE MARIE LOUIS DE LAMARTINE,
Premières Méditations Poétiques

O insupportable and touching loss!

—WILLIAM SHAKESPEARE, *Julius Caesar*

In this sad world of ours, sorrow comes to all; and, to the young, it comes with bitterest agony, because it takes them unawares. The older have learned to ever expect it.

—ABRAHAM LINCOLN, in a letter to
Fanny McCullough, Dec. 23, 1862.

Oh, to be a stone! To feel no grief!

—EURIPIDES

The pain of love lasts a lifetime

It is explained that all relationships require a little give and take. This is untrue. Any partnership demands that we give and give and give and at the last, as we flop into our graves exhausted, we are told that we didn't give enough.

—QUENTIN CRISP

Happiness in marriage is entirely a matter of chance.

—JANE AUSTEN

People who boast of happy marriages are, I submit, usually self-deceivers, if not actually liars.

—IRIS MURDOCH, *The Black Prince*

Before marriage, a man will go home and lie awake all night thinking about something you said; after marriage, he'll go to sleep before you finish saying it.

—HELEN ROWLAND, "First Interlude," *A Guide to Men*

Men marry because they are tired; women because they are curious. Both are disappointed.

—OSCAR WILDE, *A Woman of No Importance*

Divorce is the psychological equivalent of a triple coronary bypass.

—MARY KAY BLAKELY, *American Mom: Motherhood, Politics and Humble Pie*

All other woes a woman bears are minor.
But lose her husband!—might as well be dead.

—EURIPIDES, *Andromache*

Where and to whom
you are married I can only guess
in my piecemeal fashion. I grow old on my
  bitterness.

—ANNE SEXTON, "Two Sons"

It's afterwards you realize that the feeling of happiness you had with a man didn't necessarily prove that you loved him.

—MARGUERITE DURAS

How do you know love is gone? If you said that you would be there at seven and you get there by nine, and he or she has not called the police—it's gone.

—MARLENE DIETRICH

I hated her now with a hatred more fatal than indifference because it was the other side of love.

—AUGUST STRINDBERG

Lord, I don't think no man's love can last.
They love you to death then treat you like a
      thing of the past.

—BESSIE SMITH, "Dirty No-Gooder's Blues"

There's nothing worse than rejection. It's worse than death. I would wish sometimes for the guy to die because at least then I could go to his grave and visit.

—Oprah Winfrey

It is obviously quite difficult to be no longer loved when we are still in love, but it is incomparably more painful to be loved when we ourselves no longer love.

—Georges Courteline,
La Philosophie de G. Courteline

Pleasure of love lasts but a moment,
Pain of love lasts a lifetime.

—Jean Pierre Claris de Florian, French poet,
Célestine

The loss of love is a terrible thing;
They lie who say that death is worse.

—COUNTEE CULLEN, "Variations on a Theme (The
Loss of Love)," *On These I Stand*

Sad. Nothing more than sad. Let's not call it a tragedy; a broken heart is never a tragedy. Only untimely death is a tragedy.

—ANGELA CARTER, British novelist, *Wise Children*

The heart is forever inexperienced.

—HENRY DAVID THOREAU, *A Week on the Concord and
Merrimack Rivers*

Love is a tyrant sparing none

Love is a perky little elf dancing a merry little jig, and then suddenly he turns on you with a miniature machine gun.

—MATT GROENING, cartoonist

Love is a tyrant sparing none.

—PIERRE CORNEILLE, French playwright, *Le Cid*

Romance, like the rabbit at the dog track, is the elusive, fake, and never attained reward which, for the benefit and amusement of our masters, keeps us running and thinking in safe circles.

—BEVERLY JONES, feminist writer, *The Dynamics of Marriage and Motherhood*

Soul mates only exist in the Hallmark aisle of Duane Reade Drugs.

—MIRANDA (Cynthia Nixon), *Sex and the City*, written by Cindy Chupak, et al.

Why would I pay $20 to go to a strip club when I can be ignored by real women at any coffee shop for a mere $3 to $5 depending on whether I get a muffin.

—ANONYMOUS, a ThinkGeek.com customer

Nothing takes the taste out of peanut butter quite like unrequited love.

—CHARLIE BROWN, *Peanuts*, written by
Charles M. Schulz

That's the nature of women not to love when we love them, and to love when we love them not.

—MIGUEL DE CERVANTES

Men have suffered for love, and men have accomplished great feats in the name of love, but what man has ever felt at the top of his masculine form when he is lovesick or suffering from heartache?

—SUSAN BROWNMILLER, "Emotion"

Every little girl knows about love. It is only her capacity to suffer because of it that increases.

—FRANCOISE SAGAN

Sometimes I wonder if men and women really suit each other. Perhaps they should live next door and just visit now and then.

—KATHARINE HEPBURN

There is simply no dignified way for a woman to live alone. Oh, she can get along financially perhaps (though not nearly as well as a man), but emotionally she is never left in peace. Her friends, her family, her fellow workers never let her forget that her husbandlessness, her child-lessness—her selfishness, in short—is a reproach to the American way of life.

—ERICA JONG

I looked up at myself in the mirror, looking like something the cat hadn't even bothered to bring in.

—ANONYMOUS

A single woman who has never married sometimes wishes she could carry a document around
which would verify the fact that at least someone
asked her.

—HELEN GURLEY BROWN

God created man, and finding him not sufficiently
alone, gave him a companion to feel his solitude
more keenly.

—PAUL VALERY, French poet, *Tel Quel*

If only one could tell true love from false love as
one can tell mushrooms from toadstools.

—KATHERINE MANSFIELD, British author

Love is a fire. But whether it is going to warm your hearth or burn down your house, you can never tell.

—JOAN CRAWFORD

We are afraid to care too much; for fear that the other person does not care at all.

—ELEANOR ROOSEVELT

It's the heart afraid of breaking that never learns to dance.

—BETTE MIDLER

Oh, what lies lurk in kisses!

The sweeter the apple, the blacker the core. Scratch a lover and find a foe.

—Dorothy Parker

Women might be able to fake orgasms. But men can fake whole relationships.

—Sharon Stone

You have to be very fond of men. Very, very fond. You have to be very fond of them to love them. Otherwise they're simply unbearable.

—MARGUERITE DURAS

His mother should have thrown him away and kept the stork.

—MAE WEST

Don't waste time trying to break a man's heart; be satisfied if you can just manage to chip it in a brand new place.

—HELEN ROWLAND

Heav'n has no Rage like Love to Hatred turn'd, Nor Hell a Fury, like a Woman scorn'd.

—WILLIAM CONGREVE, *The Mourning Bride*

A broken heart is what makes life so wonderful five years later, when you see the guy in an elevator and he is fat and smoking a cigar and saying long-time-no-see.

—PHYLLIS BATTELLE, journalist

It serves me right for putting all my eggs in one bastard.

—DOROTHY PARKER

We shall find no fiend in hell can match the fury of a disappointed woman,—scorned, slighted, dismissed without a parting pang

—COLLEY CIBBER, British dramatist, *Love's Last Shift*

Some people wear their heart up on their sleeve.
I wear mine underneath my right pant leg, strapped
to my boot.

—ANI DIFRANCO, songwriter, singer

Boys frustrate me. I hate all their indirect messages,
I hate game playing. Do you like me or don't you?
Just tell me so I can get over you.

—KIRSTEN DUNST, actor

If you're going to burn, burn.
If you're going to boil, boil
and if you're breaking, O Heart,
go ahead and break,
for I've just left him,
that no-good man.

—HLA STAVHANA, South Indian king and poet

...I never thought of anything but a long full life with my love, but a heavy foreboding hit me about two years into this planned bliss, when he said firmly that we must never go back to the fishing village where we had spent our first Christmas.

—M.F.K. FISHER, *The Sophisticated Traveler*

He left a bad taste in my mind.

—GERALDINE ENDSOR JEWSBURY, British novelist

I know I am but summer to your heart, and not the full four seasons of the year.

—EDNA ST. VINCENT MILLAY

Tomorrow, I'll think of some way to get him back. After all, tomorrow is another day.

—Margaret Mitchell, *Gone With the Wind*

I give you my brow which you brutalized in such a cowardly way. Perhaps your kisses will revive my love. I doubt it.

—Sarah Bernhard

I buy women shoes and they use them to walk away from me.

—Mickey Rooney

I never hated a man enough to give him his diamonds back.

—Zsa Zsa Gabor

There are only three things to be done with a woman. You can love her, suffer her, or turn her into literature.

—Lawrence Durrell, *Justine*

There's not a game in the world you can play without the risk of getting hurt some.

—Katharine Hepburn

A man may be guilty of stealing a girl's heart, but he always feels hurt and indignant if she refuses to take it back again after he has finished with it.

—Helen Rowland

If you're a woman living you've been done wrong by a man.

—Oprah Winfrey

It is normal to want to ram his car if he and his new girlfriend have been spotted in it.

—HELEN LEDERER, comedian

When will I understand that what's astonishing about the number of men who remain faithful is not that it's so small but that there are any of them at all?

—NORA EPHRON

Women's hearts are like old china, none the worse for a break or two.

—W. SOMERSET MAUGHAM, *Lady Frederick*

I have loved badly, loved the great
Too soon, withdrawn my words too late
And eaten in an echoing hall
Alone and from a chipped plate
The words that I withdrew too late.

—EDNA ST. VINCENT MILLAY, "Theme and Variations,"
Huntsman, What Quarry?

To find oneself jilted is a blow to one's pride. One must do one's best to forget and if one doesn't succeed, at least one must pretend to.

—MOLIÈRE, *Tartuffe*

Books, places, amusements, people—how meaningless they become when we suspect that the person we love loves someone else!

—GERALD BRENNAN,
Thoughts in a Dry Season: A Miscellany

Love is not always blind and there are few things that cause greater wretchedness than to love with all your heart someone who you know is unworthy of love.

—W. SOMERSET MAUGHAM, *The Summing Up*

Oh what lies lurk in kisses!

—HEINRICH HEINE

It is the middle of the night and time passes...

Sometimes when I'm lonely
Don't know why,
Keep thinkin' I won't be lonely
By and by.

—LANGSTON HUGHES, "Hope [1]"

The moon has set, and the Pleiades; it is the middle of the night and time passes, time passes, and I lie alone.

—SAPPHO, "Loneliness"

Let us go in; the fog is rising.

—Attributed to EMILY DICKINSON

What makes loneliness an anguish
Is not that I have no one to share my burden
But this:
I have only my own burden to bear.

—DAG HAMMARSKJÖLD, "Markings"

Lack of money means discomfort, means squalid worries…means ever-present consciousness of failure-above all, it means loneliness.

—GEORGE ORWELL, *Keep the Aspidistra Flying*

I lie here buried alive in my loneliness.

—FRIEDRICH NIETZSCHE, *My Sister and I*

Turn up the lights; I don't want to go home in the dark.

—O. HENRY

The bottomless bitter misery of childhood: how little even now it is understood. Probably no adult misery can be compared with a child's despair.

—IRIS MURDOCH, *A Word Child*

Lord save us all from old age and broken health and a hope tree that has lost the faculty of putting out blossoms.

—MARK TWAIN, in a letter to Joe T. Goodman, April, 1891

Time doesn't heal all wounds… Over the years the scars hurt as much as the wounds.

—MARLENE DIETRICH

Who, except the gods, can live time through forever without any pain?

—Aeschylus

I answer this heroic question "Death, where is thy sting?" with "It is here in my heart and mind and memories."

—Maya Angelou,
Wouldn't Take Nothing for My Journey Now

Take this sorrow to thy heart, and make it a part of thee, and it shall nourish thee till thou art strong again.

—Henry Wadsworth Longfellow, *Hyperion*

Melancholy days…

The melancholy days are come, the saddest of
the year,
Of wailing winds, and naked woods, and
meadows brown and sere.

—WILLIAM CULLEN BRYANT,
"The Death of the Flowers"

Our life is March weather, savage and serene in
one hour.

—RALPH WALDO EMERSON, "Compensation,"
Essays: First Series

It always looks darkest just before it gets totally black.

—CHARLIE BROWN, *Peanuts*, Charles M. Schulz

When the tide of misfortune moves over you, even jelly will break your teeth.

—PERSIAN PROVERB

Part of every misery is, so to speak, the misery's shadow or reflection: the fact that you don't merely suffer but have to keep on thinking about the fact that you suffer. I not only live each endless day in grief, but live each day thinking about living each day in grief.

—C.S. LEWIS, *A Grief Observed*

Every man has his secret sorrows which the world knows not, and oftentimes we call a man cold when he is only sad.

—HENRY WADSWORTH LONGFELLOW

In middle age we are apt to reach the horrifying conclusion that all sorrow, all pain, all passionate regret and loss and bitter disillusionment are self-made.

——KATHLEEN NORRIS, author

The stabbing horror of life is not contained in calamities and disasters, because these things wake one up and one gets very familiar and intimate with them and finally they become tame again. No, it is more like being in a hotel room in Hoboken let us say, and just enough money in one's pocket for another meal.

—HENRY MILLER, author

There are days when solitude is a heady wine that intoxicates you with freedom, others when it is a bitter tonic and still others when it is a poison that makes you beat your head against the wall.

—COLETTE, *Earthly Paradise*

Sorrow happens, hardship happens. The hell with it; who never knew the price of happiness, will not be happy.

—YEVGENY YEVTUSHENKO, Russian poet

"Nobody Knows You When You're Down and Out"

—JIMMIE COX, songwriter

My memories of school have every girl in the class, except me, as blonde and pale as glasses of milk. This may explain my irrational, yet heartfelt hatred of Gwyneth Paltrow.

—EMMA FORREST, *novelist*

Having been unpopular in high school is not just cause for book publication.

—FRAN LEBOWITZ, *humorist*

We never taste a perfect joy; our happiest successes are mixed with sadness.

—PIERRE CORNEILLE, *French playwright,* Le Cid

There are no grounds for supposing that one can live a life without pain and sadness, but is it wrong to believe that somehow, somewhere, this is possible?

—HUBERT BUTLER, *"Aunt Harriet,"* The Art of the *Personal Essay*, Phillip Lopate, editor

Most of our misfortunes are more supportable than the comments of our friends upon them.

—CHARLES CALEB COLTON, English clergyman, *Lacon*

A minute to smile and an hour to weep in,
A pint of joy to a peck of trouble,
And never a laugh but the moans come double:
And that is life.

—PAUL DUNBAR, *"Life,"* The Complete Poems

Make less the depth of grief

There is some joy in weeping. For our tears
Fill up the cup, then wash our pain away.

—Ovid

To weep is to make less the depth of grief.

—William Shakespeare, *Henry VI*

Have a good cry, wash out your heart.

If you keep it inside it'll tear you apart.

Sometimes you lose, but you're gonna win if you
just hang in.

—"Better Love Next Time," Dr. Hook

Tears are the silent language of grief.

—Voltaire

A tear dries quickly, especially when it is shed for
the troubles of others.

—Charles Caleb Colton, English clergyman, *Lacon*

She was past weeping, wrapped in the ineffable
solitude of grief.

—Lady Mabell Airlie, speaking of Queen Mary
as she watched the funeral procession of
her son King George VI

But, truly, I have wept too much! The dawns are heartbreaking. Every moon is atrocious and every sun bitter.

—ARTHUR RIMBAUD, "Le Bateau Ivre"

If you suppress grief too much it can well redouble.

—MOLIÈRE, French playwright

Give sorrow words: the grief that does not speak
Whispers the o'er-fraught heart and bids it break.

—WILLIAM SHAKESPEARE, *Macbeth*

One often calms one's grief by recounting it.

—PIERRE CORNEILLE, French playwright

If thou shouldst never see my face again,
Pray for my soul. More things are wrought
    by prayer
Than this world dreams of.

—ALFRED, LORD TENNYSON, "The Passing of Arthur "

If it were not for hopes, the heart would break

—THOMAS FULLER, M.D., *Gnomologia*

Let mourning stop when one's grief is fully expressed.

—CONFUCIUS

Company loves misery

When you are in trouble, people who call to sympathize are really looking for the particulars.

—EDGAR WATSON HOWE, *Country Town Sayings*

Of all cruelties those are the most intolerable that come under the name of condolence and consolation.

—WALTER SAVAGE LANDOR, in a letter to
Robert Southey, 1816

You may regret calamities if you can thereby help the sufferer, but if you cannot, mind your own business.

—RALPH WALDO EMERSON, Journals

Why not leave their private sorrows to people? Is sorrow not, one asks, the only thing in the world people really possess?

—VLADIMIR NABOKOV, Pnin

How often could things be remedied by a word. How often it is left unspoken.

—NORMAN DOUGLAS, An Almanac

Count on it, if a person talks of their misfortune, there is something in it that is not disagreeable to them.

—SAMUEL JOHNSON, English essayist

To weep excessively for the dead is to affront the living.

—THOMAS FULLER, M.D., *Gnomologia*

Perhaps the worst thing about suffering is that it finally hardens the hearts of those around it.

—GLORIA STEINEM,
Outrageous Acts and Everyday Rebellions

Sometimes you have a friend and you think they are made of rock, and suddenly you realize they're only made of sand.

—MARIA CALLAS

You got a lotta nerve
To say you are my friend.
When I was down
You just stood there grinning.

—BOB DYLAN, "Positively 4th Street"

Easy for you to say...

"Your handkerchief is to wave, not to cry into."

—Princess Elizabeth, cautioning her sister,
Princess Margaret, as they said farewell
to their parents

It is foolish to tear one's hair in grief, as though sorrow would be made less by baldness.

—Cicero

The young widow...should, of course, never remain in mourning for her first husband after she has decided to be consoled by a second.

—EMILY POST

You may not know it, but at the far end of despair, there is a white clearing where one is almost happy.

—JEAN ANOUILH, *Restless Heart*

That which does not kill me makes me stronger.

—NIETZSCHE, *Twilight of the Idols*

Unhappiness does make people look stupid.

—ANATOLE FRANCE, *The Crime of Sylvestre Bonnard*

Try the Lamentations of Jeremiah. They always pick me up.

—PETER DE VRIES, in a letter to Paul Theroux

Melancholy cannot be clearly proved to others, so it is better to be silent about it.

—JAMES BOSWELL, *London Journal*

The world is quickly bored by the recital of misfortune, and willingly avoids the sight of distress.

—W. SOMERSET MAUGHAM, *The Moon and Sixpence*

Never bear more than one kind of trouble at a time. Some people bear three kinds; all they have had, all they have now, and all they expect to have.

—EDWARD EVERETT HALE, Unitarian clergyman

If you are distressed by anything external, the pain is not due to the thing itself but your own estimate of it; and this you have the power to revoke at any moment.

—MARCUS AURELIUS, *Meditations*

Happiness is beneficial for the body, but it is grief that develops the powers of the mind.

—MARCEL PROUST,
Remembrance of Things Past: The Past Recaptured

So long as we can lose any happiness, we possess some.

—BOOTH TARKINGTON,
Looking Forward to the Great Adventure

There is no joy but calm.

—ALFRED, LORD TENNYSON, "The Lotos-Eaters"

Looking for peace is like looking for a turtle with a mustache: you won't be able to find it. But when your heart is ready, peace will come looking for you.

—AJAHN CHAH, *Reflections*

Have courage for the great sorrows of life and patience for the small ones; and when you have laboriously accomplished your daily task, go to sleep in peace.

—VICTOR HUGO, *The Hunchback of Notre Dame*

"Begin at the beginning," the King said gravely, "and go till you come to the end; then stop."

—LEWIS CARROLL, *Alice's Adventures in Wonderland*

Every cloud engenders not a storm

My life has been filled with terrible misfortune; most of which never happened.

—MICHEL DE MONTAIGNE, French philosopher

Don't tell your problems to people: eighty percent don't care; and the other twenty percent are glad you have them.

—LOU HOLTZ, football coach

Well, everybody in Casablanca has problems. Yours may work out.

—RICK (HUMPHREY BOGART), *Casablanca*, written by
Julius Epstein, Philip Epstein, and Howard Koch

Compare your griefs with other men's

Are you then unable to recognize a sob unless it has the same sound as yours?

—ANDRE GIDE, *Journals*

I measure every grief I meet with narrow, probing eyes—I wonder if it weighs like mine—or has an easier size.

—EMILY DICKINSON

Compare your griefs with other men's and they will seem less.

—SPANISH PROVERB

What we call mourning for our dead is perhaps not so much grief at not being able to call them back; as it is grief at not being able to want to do so.

—THOMAS MANN

Grief can't be shared. Everyone carries it alone, his own burden, his own way.

—ANNE MORROW LINDBERGH, *Dearly Beloved*

Everyone can master a grief but he that has it.

    —WILLIAM SHAKESPEARE, *Much Ado about Nothing*

Between grief and nothing I will take grief.

    —WILLIAM FAULKNER, *The Wild Palms*

Where grief is fresh, any attempt to divert it only irritates.

    —SAMUEL JOHNSON, English essayist

Life is made up of sobs, sniffles, and smiles, with sniffles predominating.

    —O. HENRY, "The Gift of the Magi," *The Four Million*

An hour of pain is as long as a day of pleasure.

—ENGLISH PROVERB

Grief drives men into habits of serious reflection, sharpens the understanding and softens the heart.

—JOHN ADAMS, in a letter to Thomas Jefferson,
May 6, 1816.

Man never reasons so much and becomes so introspective as when he suffers; since he is anxious to get at the cause of his sufferings, to learn who has produced them, and whether it is just or unjust that he should have to bear them.

—LUIGI PIRANDELLO,
Six Characters in Search of an Author

Laughter is wine for the soul

The human race has one really effective weapon, and that is laughter.

—Mark Twain

Laughter is wine for the soul—laughter soft, or loud and deep, tinged through with seriousness.

—Sean O'Casey, "The Power of Laughter: Weapon against Evil," *Fifty Famous Essays*

Life does not cease to be funny when people die any more than it ceases to be serious when people laugh.

—George Bernard Shaw

If life must not be taken too seriously—then so neither must death.

—Samuel Butler, "Death," *Note-Books*

There is no cure for birth and death save to enjoy the interval.

—George Santayana

Laughter is the tonic, the relief, the surcease for pain.

—Charlie Chaplin

Life is a tragedy for those who feel; and a comedy for those who think.

—Chinese proverb

I laugh because I must not cry. That is all. That is all.

—Abraham Lincoln

And if I laugh at any mortal thing,
'Tis that I may not weep.

—Lord Byron, *Don Juan*

Your joy is your sorrow unmasked,
And the selfsame well from which your laughter rises was oftentimes filled with your tears.

—Kahlil Gibran, *The Prophet*

A merry heart goes all the day
Your sad tires in a mile-a.

—WILLIAM SHAKESPEARE, *The Winter's Tale*

I have always believed that God never gives a cross to bear larger than we can carry. No matter what, he wants us to be happy, not sad. Birds sing after a storm. Why shouldn't we?

—ROSE KENNEDY

One can bear grief, but it takes two to be glad.

—ELBERT HUBBARD, *The Note Book*

With coarse rice to eat, with water to drink, and my bent arm for a pillow—I have still joy in the midst of all these things.

—CONFUCIUS

The things we laugh at are awful while they are going on, but get funny when we look back. And other people laugh because they've been through it, too.

—JAMES THURBER, *Collecting Himself*

Life can be wildly tragic at times, and I've had my share. But whatever happens to you, you have to keep a slightly comic attitude. In the final analysis, you have got to not forget to laugh.

—KATHARINE HEPBURN

One joy scatters a hundred griefs.

—CHINESE PROVERB

Laughter is the sun that drives winter from the human face.

—VICTOR HUGO

What's the use of worrying?
It never was worthwhile,
So, pack up your troubles in your kit-bag
And smile, smile, smile.

—GEORGE ASAF, songwriter,
"Pack up Your Troubles in Your Old Kit-bag"

Gray skies are just clouds passing over

When things are bad, we take comfort in the thought that they could always get worse. And when they are, we find hope in the thought that things are so bad they have to get better.

—MALCOLM S. FORBES

Sorrow comes to all... Perfect relief is not possible, except with time. You cannot now realize that you will ever feel better and yet you are sure to be happy again.

—ABRAHAM LINCOLN

In spite of illness, in spite even of the archenemy sorrow, one can remain alive long past the usual date of disintegration if one is unafraid of change, insatiable in intellectual curiosity, interested in big things, and happy in small ways.

—EDITH WHARTON

They are surely to be esteemed the bravest spirits who, having the clearest sense of both the pains and pleasures of life, do not on that account shrink from danger.

—THUCYDIDES

Life is mostly froth and bubble,
Two things stand like stone,
Kindness in another's trouble,
Courage in your own.

—ADAM LINDSAY GORDON, "Ye Wearie Wayfarer"

At sometime in our lives a devil dwells within us, causes heartbreaks, confusion and troubles, then dies.

—THEODORE ROOSEVELT

Some misfortunes we bring upon ourselves; others are completely beyond our control. But no matter what happens to us, we always have some control over what we do about it.

—SUZY SZASZ, *Living With It: Why You Don't Have to Be Healthy to Be Happy*

It is always darkest just before the day dawneth.

—THOMAS FULLER, *A Pisgah-Sight of Palestine*

Gray skies are just clouds passing over.

—DUKE ELLINGTON

In the depth of winter, I finally learned that within me lay an invincible summer.

—ALBERT CAMUS, *L'Eté*

Courage is
the thing...

To face despair and not give in to it, that's courage.

—TED KOPPEL, journalist

Courage is the thing. All goes if courage goes.

— J. M. BARRIE

A high heart ought to bear calamities and not flee them, since in bearing them appears the grandeur of the mind and in fleeing them the cowardice of the heart.

—PIETRO ARETINO, in a letter to the King of France, April 24, 1525.

Courage is resistance to fear, mastery of fear—not absence of fear.

—MARK TWAIN, *The Tragedy of Pudd'nhead Wilson*

Sometimes it is an act of bravery even to live.

—SENECA THE YOUNGER, *Moral Letters to Lucilius*

I am not the least afraid to die.

—CHARLES DARWIN, *The Autobiography of Charles Darwin and Selected Letters*

The brave may know defeat but never despair.

—ANONYMOUS

Hold back, O my God, these torrents which over-whelm me, or else enlarge my capacity for their reception.

—MARGARET MARY ALACOQUE in William James'
*The Varieties of Religious Experience:
A Study in Human Nature*

I used to hurt so badly that I'd ask God why, what have I done to deserve any of this? I feel now He was preparing me for this, for the future. That's the way I see it.

—JANET JACKSON, entertainer

Pain makes man think. Thought makes man wise. Wisdom makes life endurable.

—John Patrick, *The Teahouse of the August Moon*

Real sorrow is incompatible with hope. No matter how great that sorrow may be, hope raises it one hundred cubits higher.

—Le Comte de Lautréamont, *Poesies*

I find life itself provides ample and sufficient tests of my valor and mettle: illness; betrayal; fruitless searches for love; working for the abusive, the insane, and the despotic. All challenges easily as thrilling to me as scrambling over icy rock in a pair of barely adequate boots.

—David Rakoff, *Fraud*

Tea and sympathy

Friendship is certainly the finest balm for the pangs of disappointed love.

—Jane Austen

The friend who can be silent with us in a moment of despair or confusion, who can stay with us in an hour of grief and bereavement, who can tolerate not knowing…not healing, not curing…that is a friend who cares.

——Henri Nouwen, Jesuit priest, psychologist

The friend who holds your hand and says the wrong thing is made of dearer stuff than the one who stays away.

—BARBARA KINGSOLVER,
High Tide in Tucson: Essays from Now or Never

Often we can help each other most by leaving each other alone; at other times we need the hand-grasp and the word of cheer.

—ELBERT HUBBARD, *The Note Book*

What value has compassion that does not take its object in its arms?

—ANTOINE DE SAINT-EXUPERY, *The Wisdom of the Sands*

Never does one feel oneself so utterly helpless as in trying to speak comfort for great bereavement. I will not try it. Time is the only comforter for the loss of a mother.

—Jane Welsh Carlyle, Scottish poet, in a letter to her husband, Thomas Carlyle, December 27, 1853

To live in the hearts we leave
Is not to die.

—Thomas Campbell, "Hallowed Ground"

I do not believe that sheer suffering teaches. If suffering alone taught, all the world would be wise, since everyone suffers. To suffering must be added mourning, understanding, patience, love, openness and the willingness to remain vulnerable.

—Anne Morrow Lindbergh

My heart, which is so full to overflowing, has often been solaced and refreshed by music when sick and weary.

—MARTIN LUTHER, leader of the
Protestant Reformation

Sorrow can be alleviated by good sleep, a bath and a glass of wine.

—ST. THOMAS AQUINAS

Noble deeds and hot baths are the best cure for depression.

—DODIE SMITH, *I Capture the Castle*

Sleep is pain's easiest salve...

—JOHN DONNE

There is nothing sweeter than to be sympathized
with.

—GEORGE SANTAYANA,
The Life of Reason: Reason in Common Sense

If you want inner peace find it in solitude, not
speed, and if you would find yourself, look to the
land from which you came and to which you go.

—STEWART UDALL, *The Quiet Crisis*

Love can heal a broken heart.

—ANONYMOUS

The best way to cheer yourself is to try to cheer somebody else up.

—MARK TWAIN, *Mark Twain's Notebook*

Fall seven times, stand up eight

Although the world is full of suffering, it is full also of the overcoming of it.

—HELEN KELLER, *Optimism*

Most of the important things in the world have been accomplished by people who have kept on trying when there seemed to be no hope at all.

—DALE CARNEGIE

I have sometimes been wildly, despairingly, acutely miserable, racked with sorrow, but through it all I still know quite certainly that just to be alive is a grand thing.

—AGATHA CHRISTIE

After sorrow comes joy.

—ARAB SAYING

Of all ills that one endures, hope is a cheap and universal cure.

—ABRAHAM COWLEY, British poet

My sun sets to rise again.

—ROBERT BROWNING, poet

Hold your head high, stick your chest out. You can make it. It gets dark sometimes, but morning comes. Keep hope alive.

—JESSE JACKSON

After darkness comes light.

—ANONYMOUS

It is said an eastern monarch once charged his wise men to invent a sentence, to be ever in view, and which should be true and appropriate in all times and situations. They presented him with the words, 'And this, too, shall pass away.' How much it expresses! How chastening in the hour of pride! How consoling in the depths of affliction!

—ABRAHAM LINCOLN

Be still my heart; thou hast known worse than this.

—HOMER

In living and in seeing other men, the heart must break or become as bronze.

—SÉBASTIEN ROCH NICOLAS CHAMFORT,
Caractères et Anecdotes

And thus the heart will break, yet brokenly live on.

—LORD BYRON, "Childe Harold's Pilgrimage"

Fall seven times, stand up eight.

—JAPANESE PROVERB

Ever'thing we do—seems to me is aimed right at going' on. Seems that way to me. Even gettin' hungry—even bein' sick; some die, but the rest is tougher.

—JOHN STEINBECK, *The Grapes of Wrath*

To endure what is unendurable is true endurance.

—JAPANESE PROVERB

Keep on truckin', mama,
Truckin' my blues away.

—ANONYMOUS, "Truckin"

Sorrow and silence are strong, and patient endurance is godlike.

—HENRY WADSWORTH LONGFELLOW, *Evangeline*

I've had heartaches, headaches, toothaches, earaches, and I've had a few pains in the ass; but I've survived to tell about it.

—DOLLY PARTON

Ah done been in sorrow's kitchen and Ah done licked out all de pots. Ah done died in grief and been buried in de bitter waters, and Ah done rose agin from de dead lak Lazarus.

—ZORA NEALE HURSTON, *Jonah's Gourd Vine*